AF595879
Hello, my name is Marlee.
About me
My name is ____________.

Track your progress

Find and trace each letter to match your completed pages.

a s o g c k e u w v x y z

as in "box"

Teacher note *As each letter page is completed, students trace the letter on this tracker.*

t
p
i
d
m
n
r
h
b
j
l
f
q
I'm hiding ...
circle me when
you find me on
the pages.

Before you begin writing ...

Posture

- Relax your arms.
- Sit back in your chair.
- Make sure your back is straight.

Put your feet flat on the floor.

Pencil grip

How you hold your pencil is important.

- Hold your pencil firmly between your thumb and index finger.
- Balance the pencil on your middle finger.
- Don't grip the pencil too tightly!

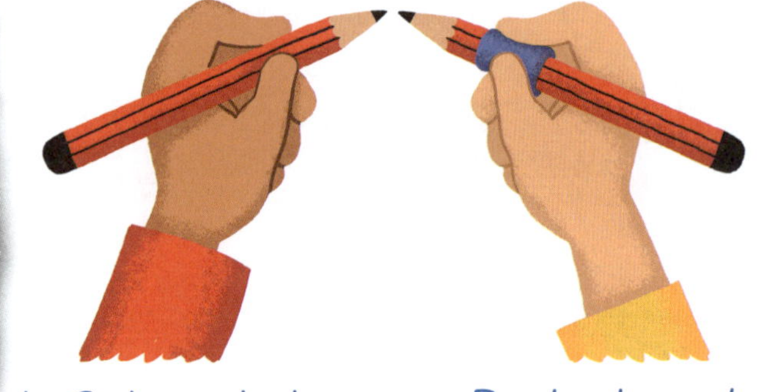

Left-handed Right-handed

Paper position

- Tilt your page.
- Use your non-writing hand to steady the paper.

Left-handed

Right-handed

Numbers

Teacher note

Correct number formation is essential in mathematics and should be as fluent and automatic as handwriting letters and words.

Warm-up patterns

Teacher note *Trace these patterns in different colours.*

Teacher note

Track the letter with a finger.
Trace the letter with a pencil.
Copy the letter with a pencil.

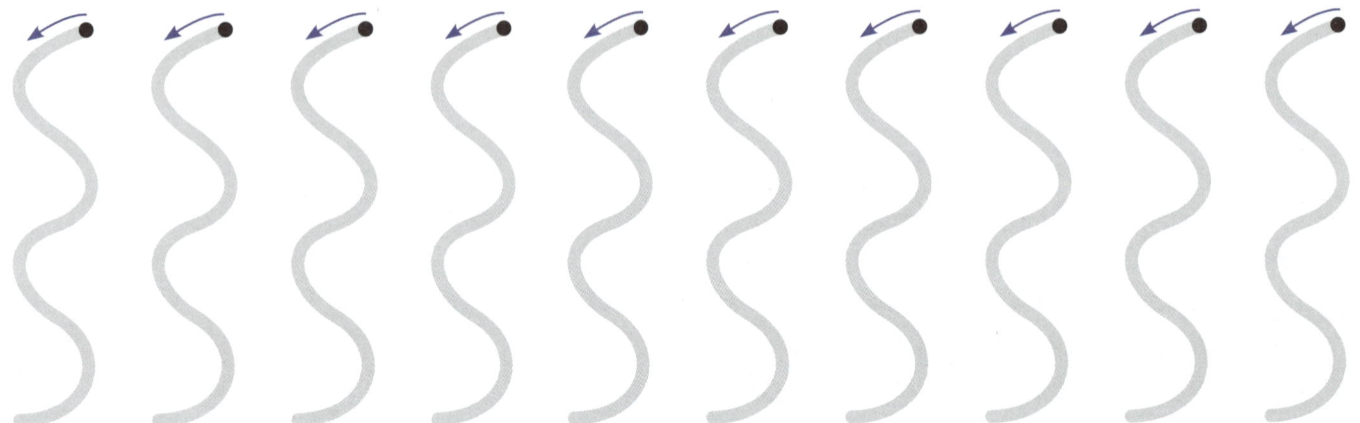

Track

Trace

Copy

Self-assessment!

Ask students to circle their best lower-case s and upper-case S.
Ask them to explain the reason for their choices to you or a classmate.

Fast finishers

Draw a picture of something beginning with the /s/ phoneme (sound), e.g. the Sun.

Track

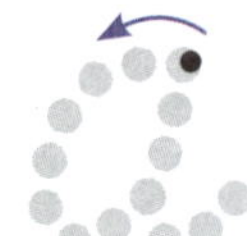    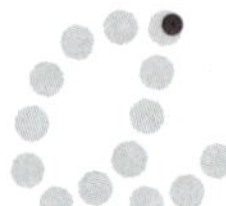 

Trace

Copy

Self-assessment!

Ask students to circle their best lower-case a and upper-case A.
Ask them to explain the reason for their choices to you or a classmate.

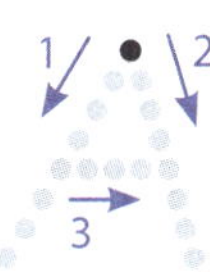

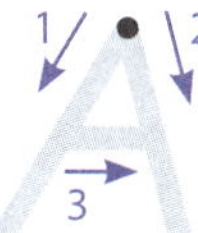

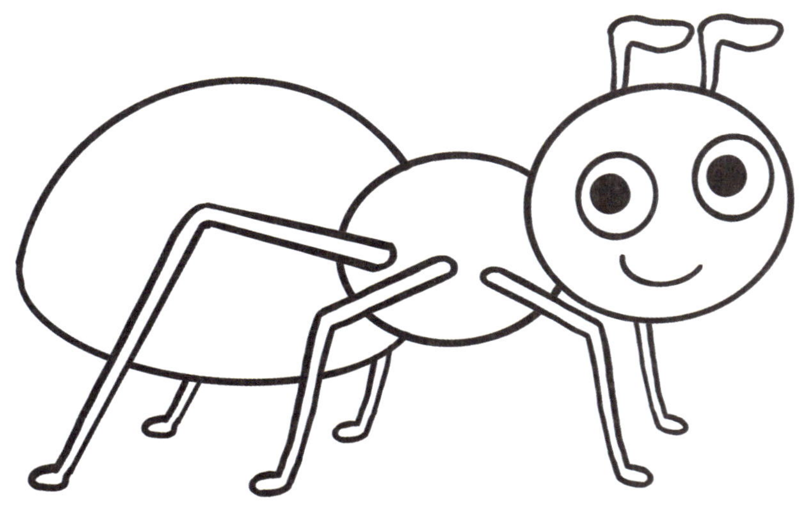

Fast finishers Trace over the letter a, and then colour in the picture of the ant.

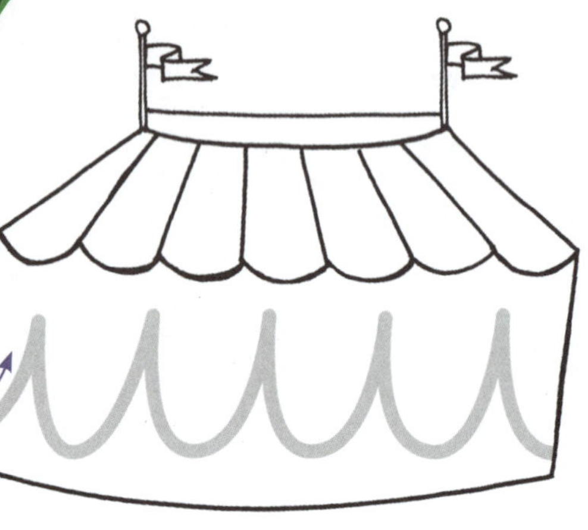

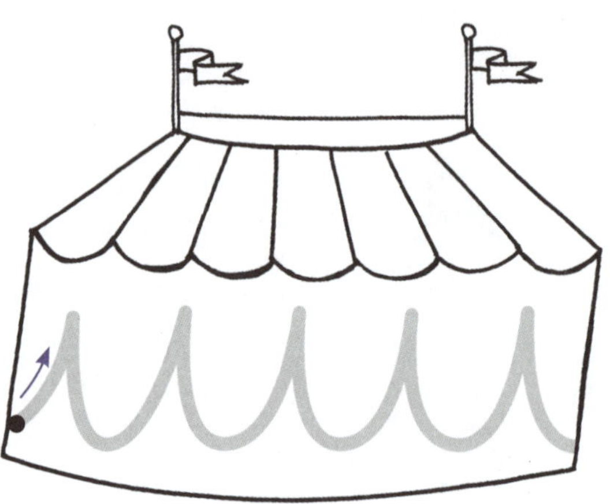

Track

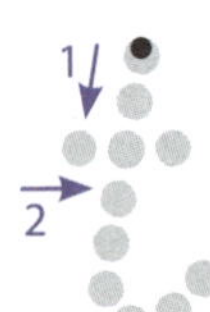     

Trace

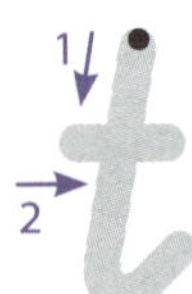     

Copy

Self-assessment!

Ask students to circle their best lower-case t and upper-case T.
Ask them to explain the reason for their choices to you or a classmate.

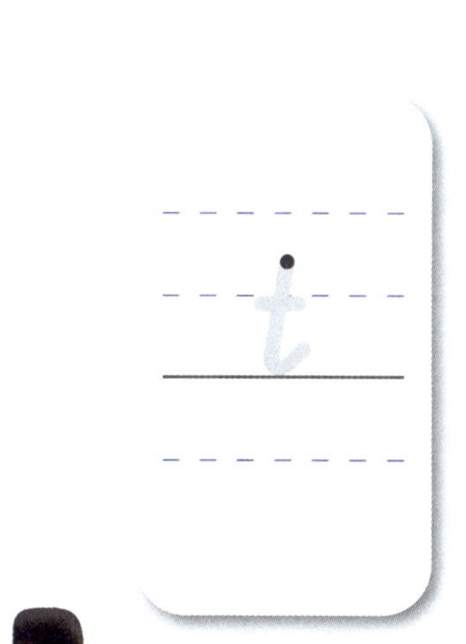

Fast finishers

Trace over the letter t, and then colour in the picture of a tap.

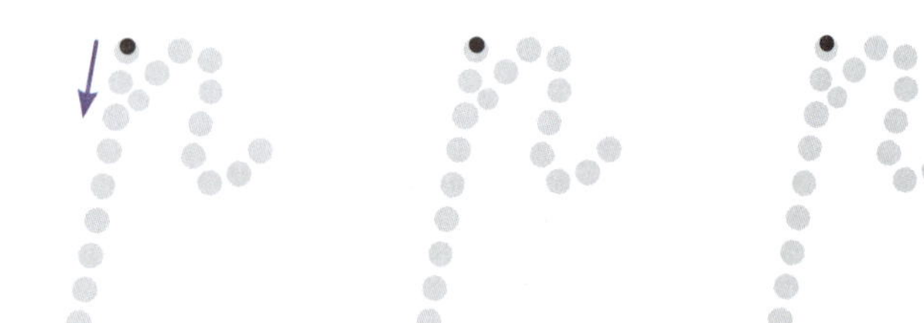

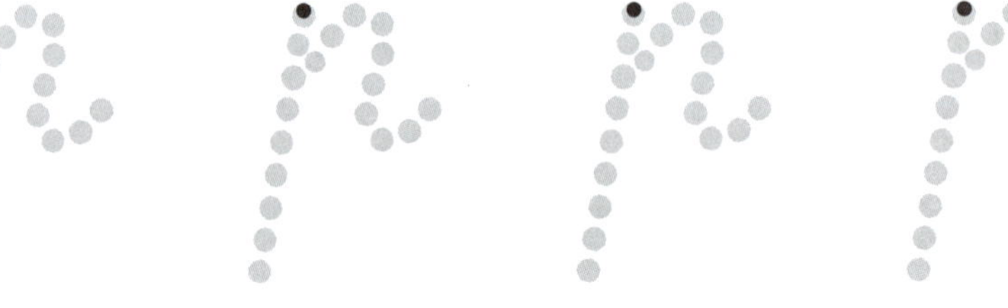

Track

Trace

Copy

Self-assessment!

Ask students to circle their best lower-case p and upper-case P.
Ask them to explain the reason for their choices to you or a classmate.

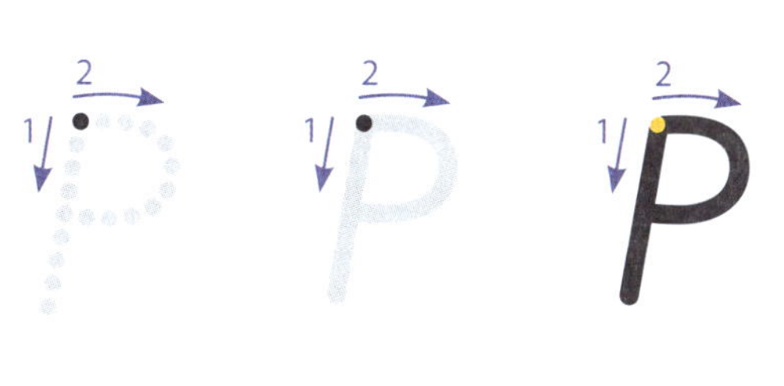

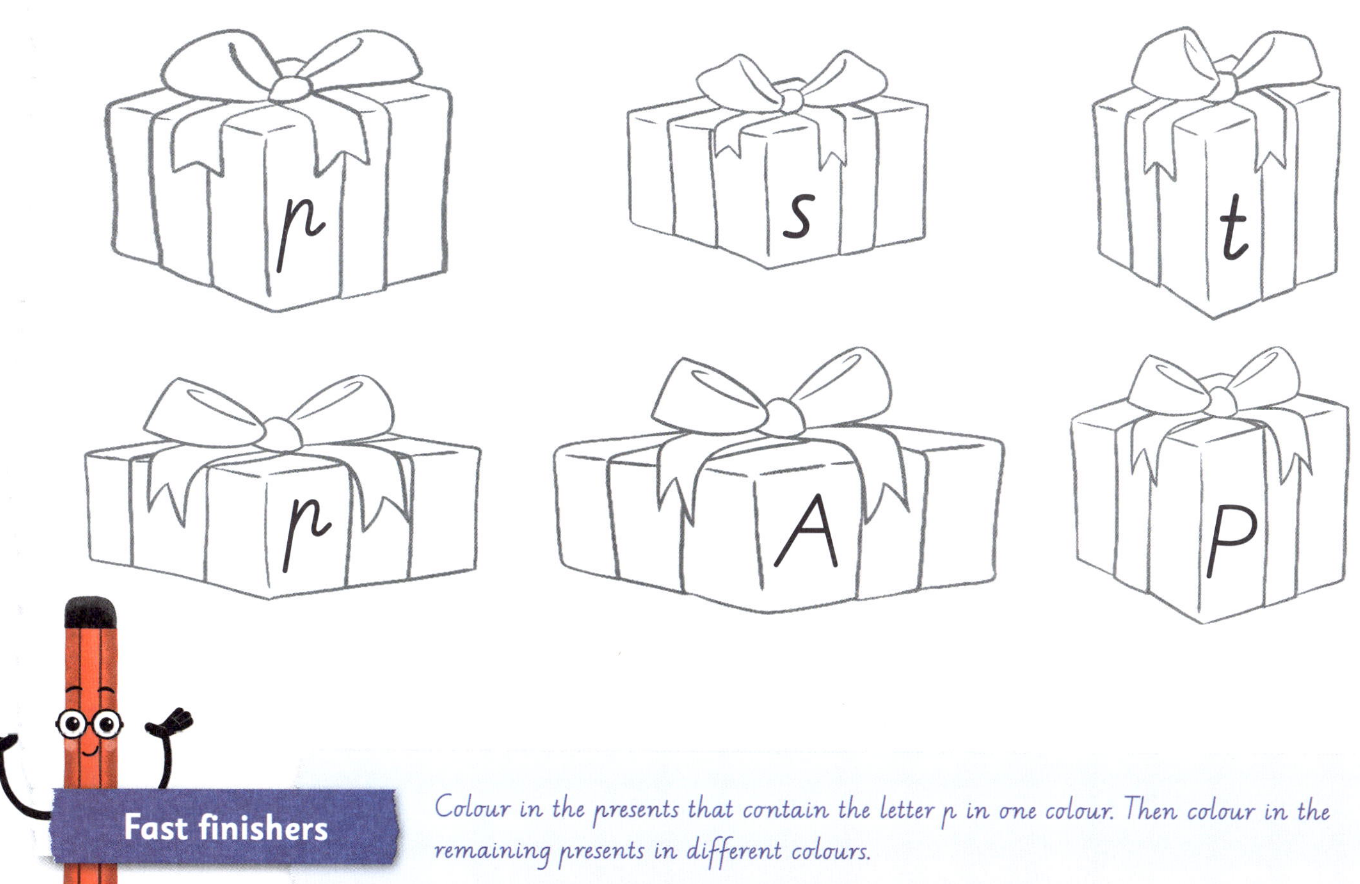

Fast finishers

Colour in the presents that contain the letter p in one colour. Then colour in the remaining presents in different colours.

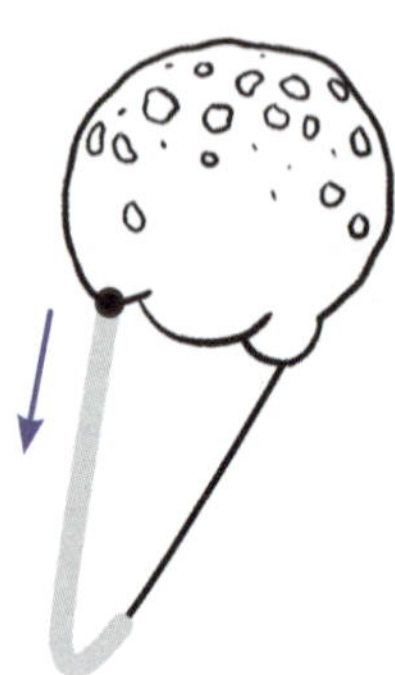
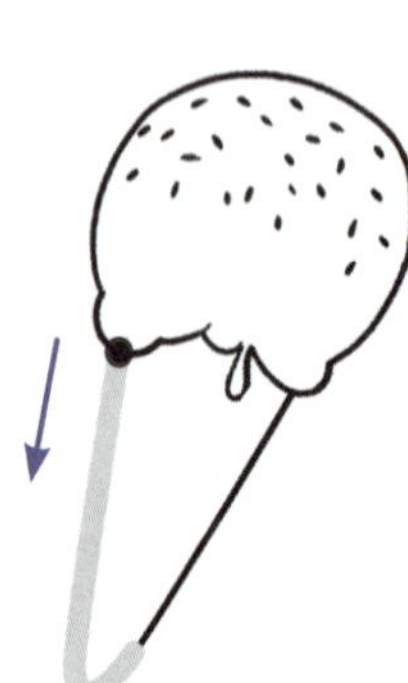
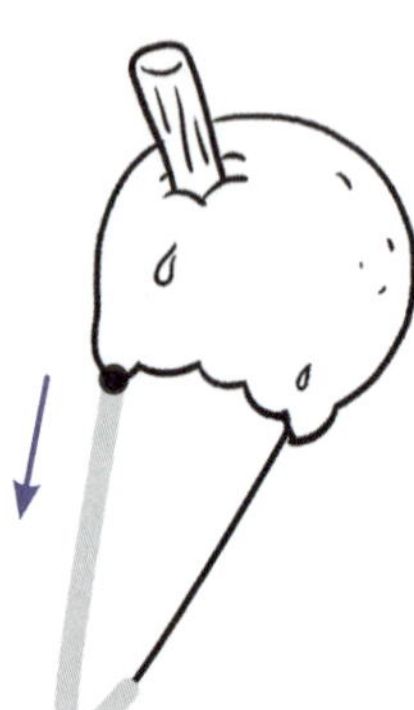
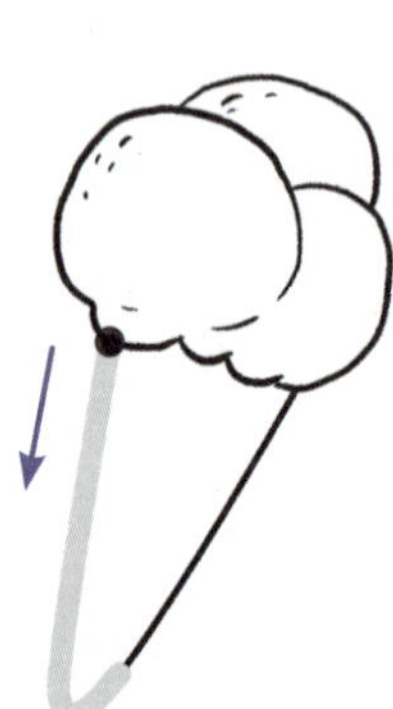

Track

Trace

Copy

Self-assessment!

Ask students to circle their best lower-case i and upper-case I.
Ask them to explain the reason for their choices to you or a classmate.

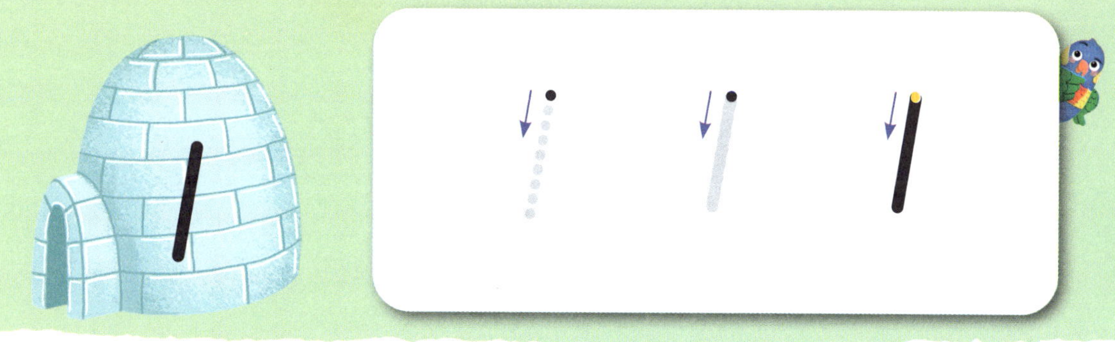

s i i a i

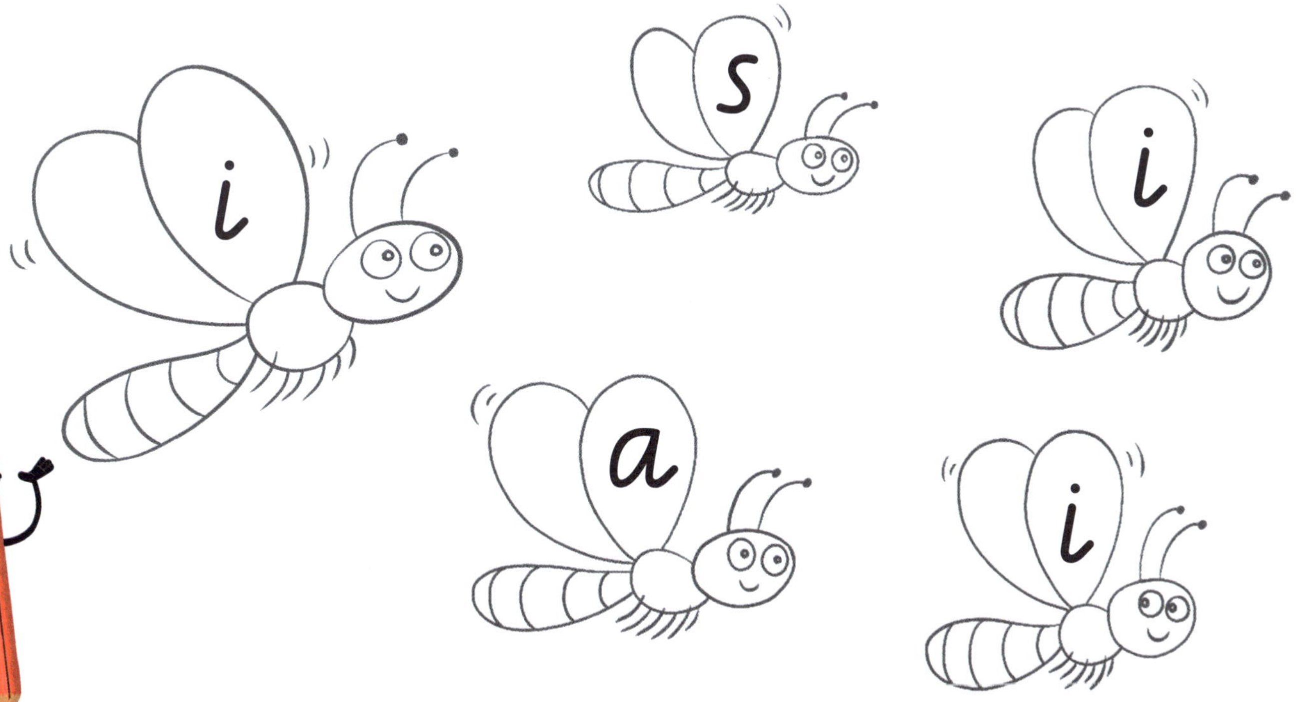

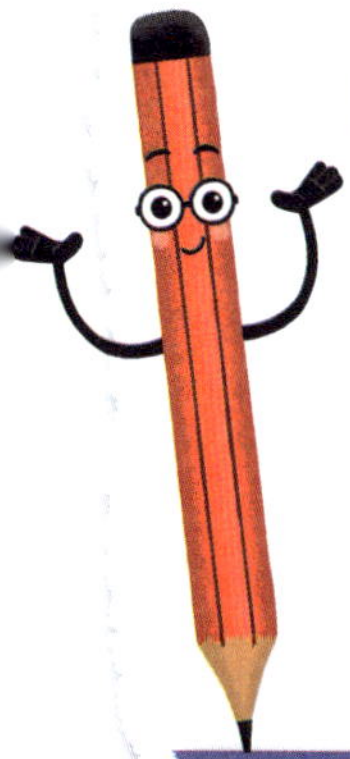

Fast finishers

Colour in the insects that contain a lower-case i in one colour. Then colour in the remaining insects in different colours.

Track

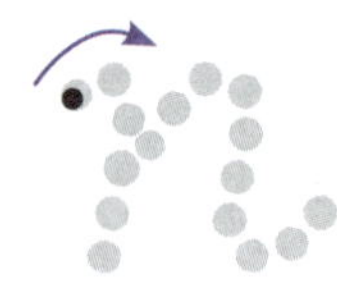

Trace

Copy

Self-assessment!

Ask students to circle their best lower-case n and upper-case N.
Ask them to explain the reason for their choices to you or a classmate.

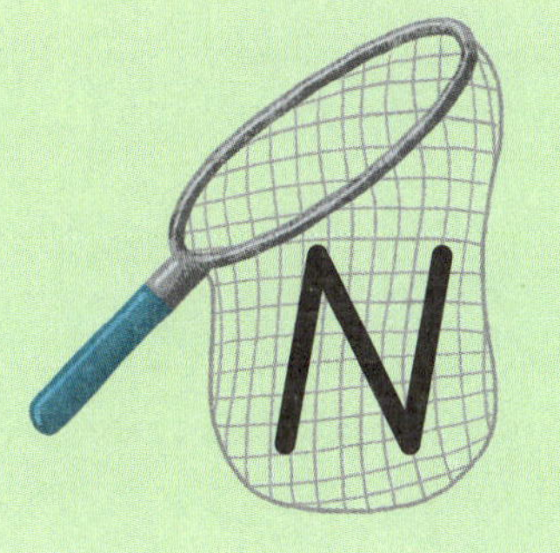

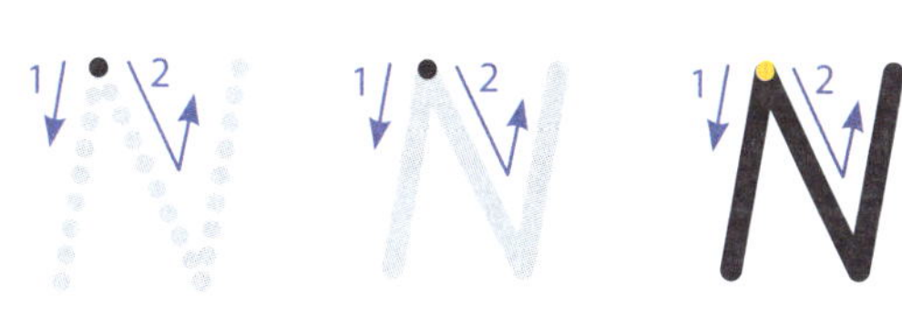

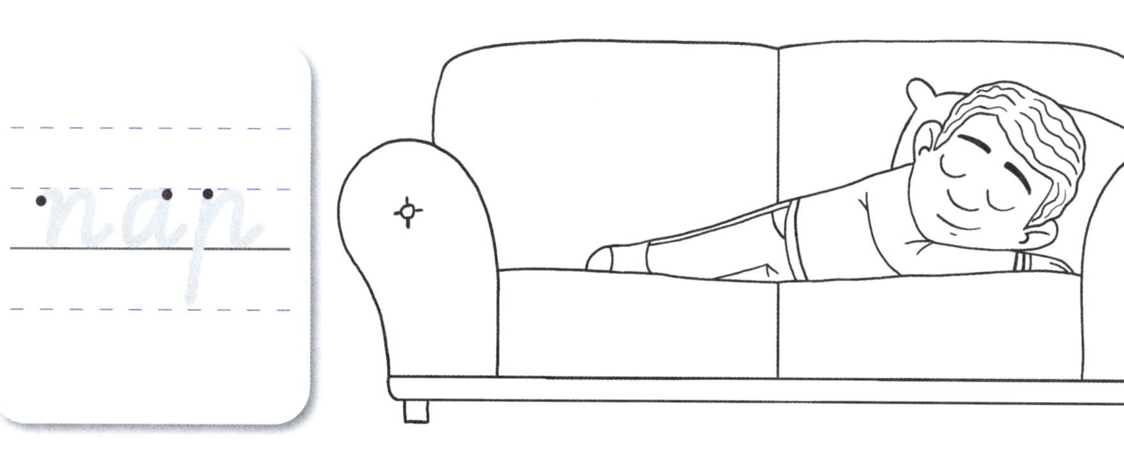

Fast finishers

Trace over the word "nap", and then colour in the picture of the child having a nap.

Track

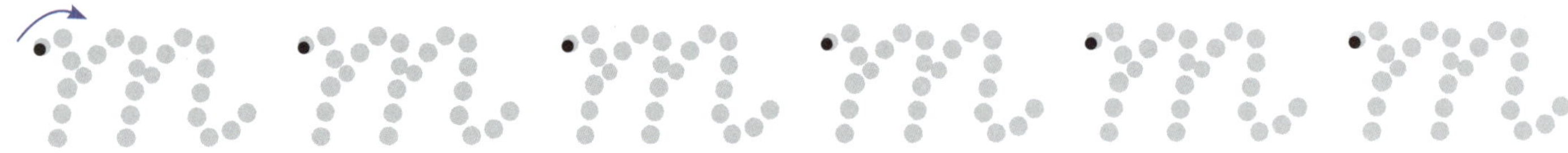

Trace

m m m m m m

Copy

Self-assessment!

Ask students to circle their best lower-case m and upper-case M.
Ask them to explain the reason for their choices to you or a classmate.

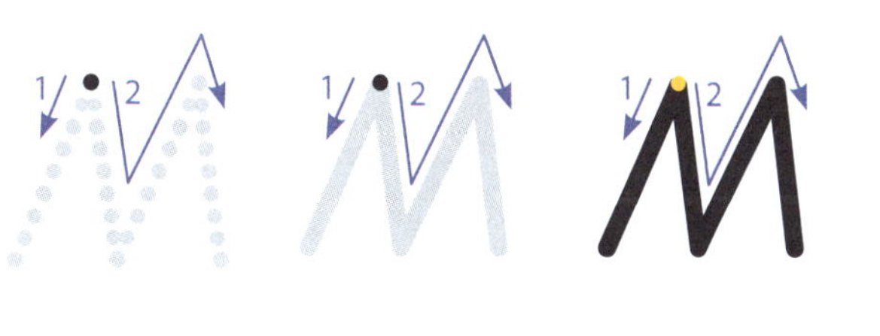

Fast finishers

Trace over the word "map", and then colour in the map.

Track

Trace

Copy

Self-assessment!

Ask students to circle their best lower-case d and upper-case D.
Ask them to explain the reason for their choices to you or a classmate.

above
on
below
D

above
on
below
D

above
on
below
d

above
on
below
d

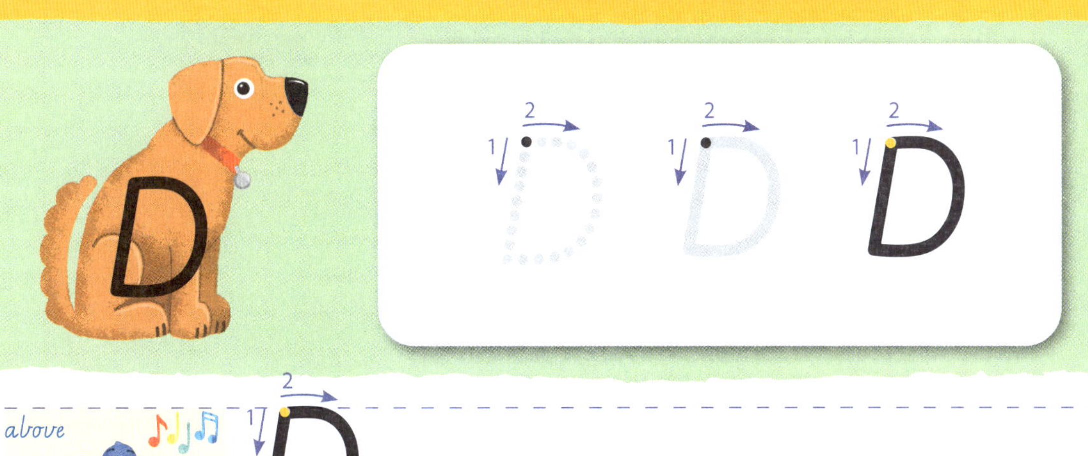

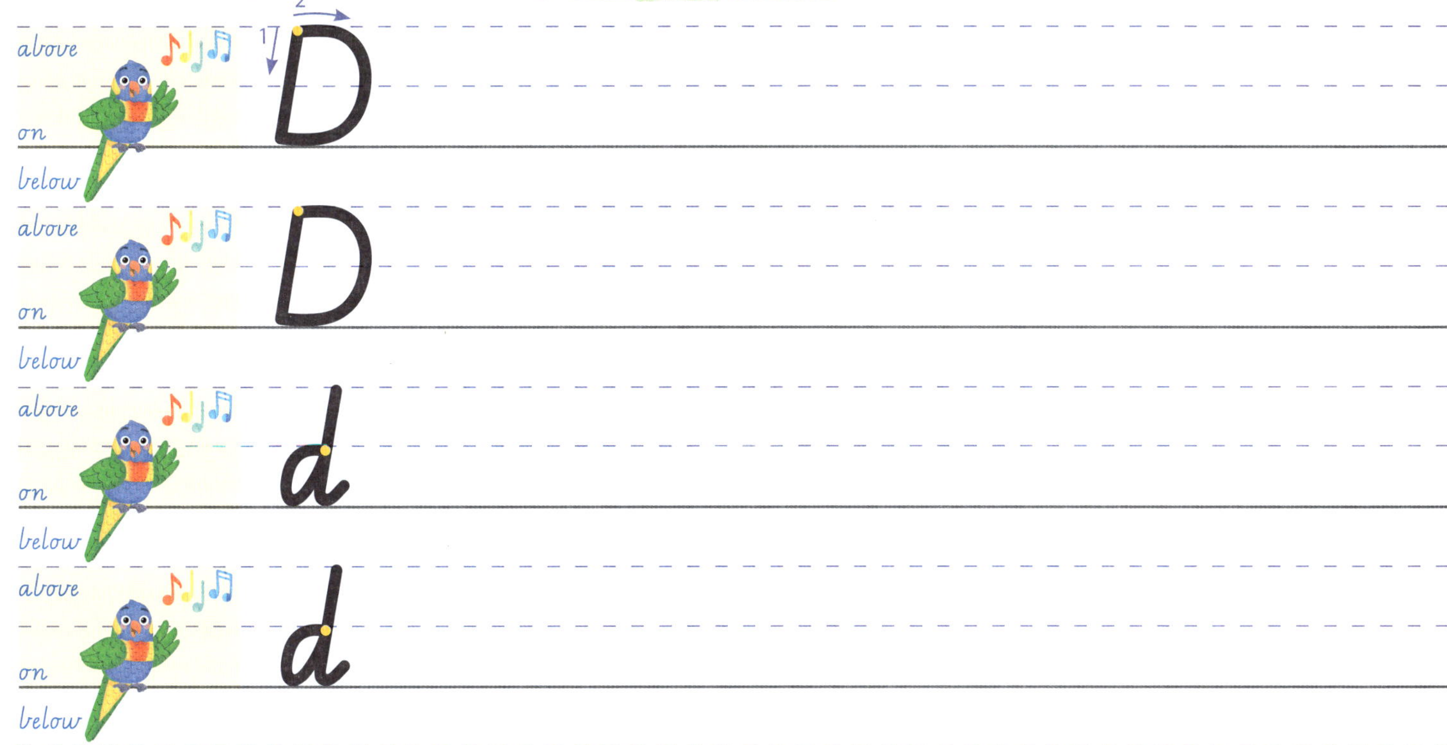

Sam Dad

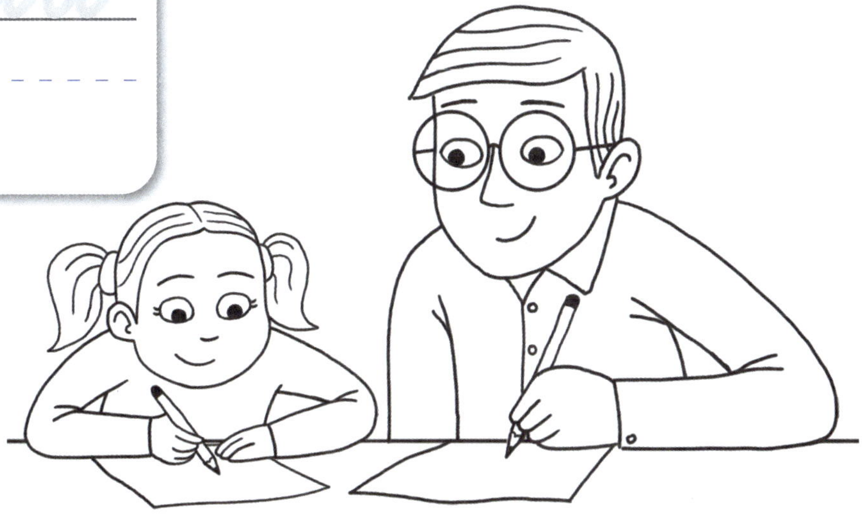

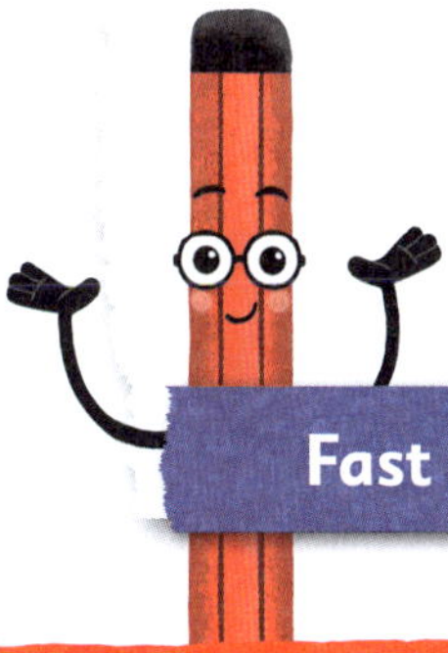

Fast finishers

Trace over the names, and then colour in the drawing of Sam and her dad.

Track

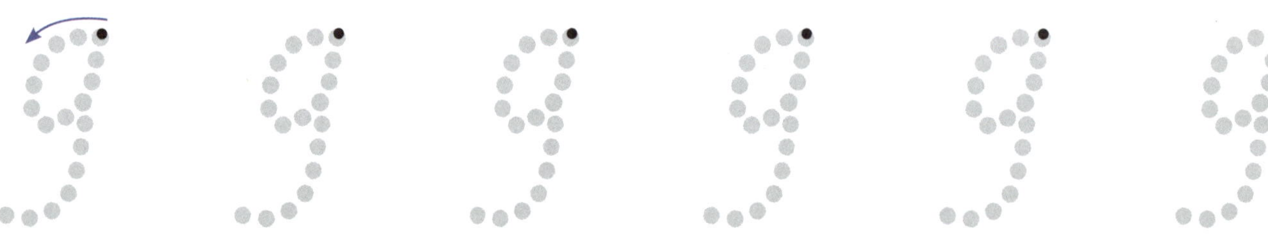

Trace

Copy

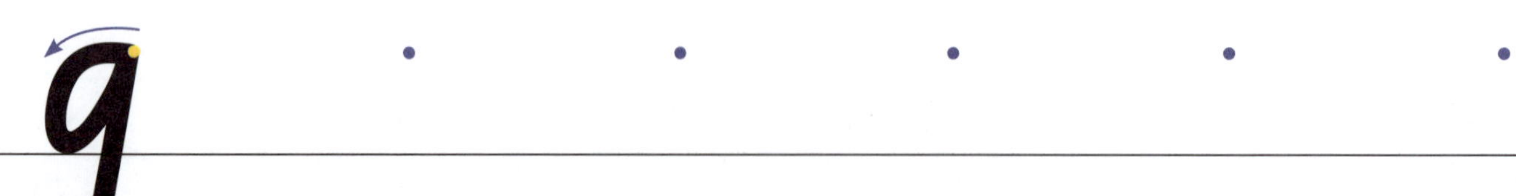

Self-assessment! Ask students to circle their best lower-case g and upper-case G. Ask them to explain the reason for their choices to you or a classmate.

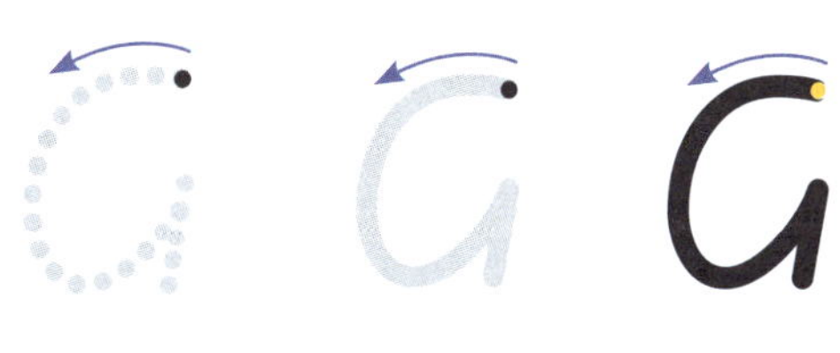

g s t i g

Fast finishers

Colour in the flowerpots that contain a lower-case g in one colour. Then colour in the remaining flowerpots in different colours.

Track

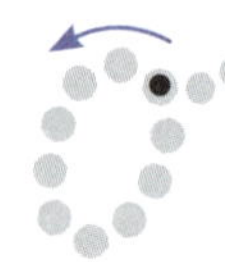     

Trace

Copy

Self-assessment!

Ask students to circle their best lower-case o and upper-case O.
Ask them to explain the reason for their choices to you or a classmate.

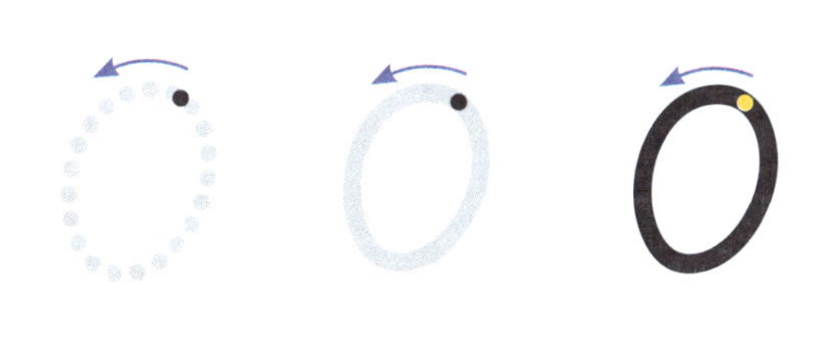

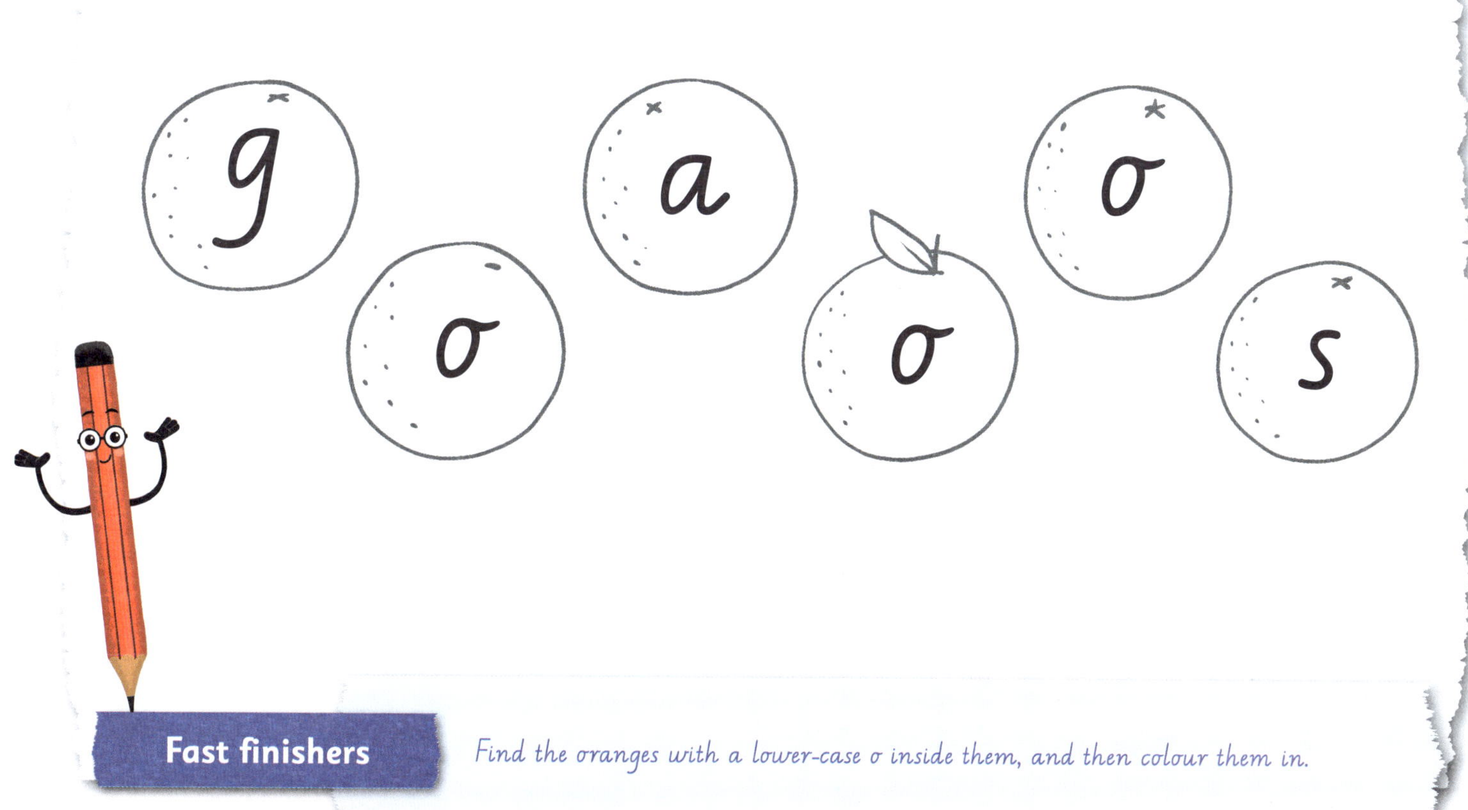

Fast finishers Find the oranges with a lower-case o inside them, and then colour them in.

Track

     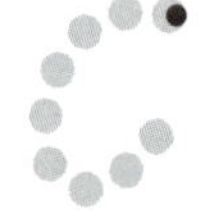

Trace

Copy

Self-assessment!

Ask students to circle their best lower-case c and upper-case C.
Ask them to explain the reason for their choices to you or a classmate.

above
on
below

above
on
below

above
on
below

above
on
below

Fast finishers Trace the word "can", and then draw something you can do.

Track

Trace

Copy

Self-assessment! Ask students to circle their best lower-case k and upper-case K. Ask them to explain the reason for their choices to you or a classmate.

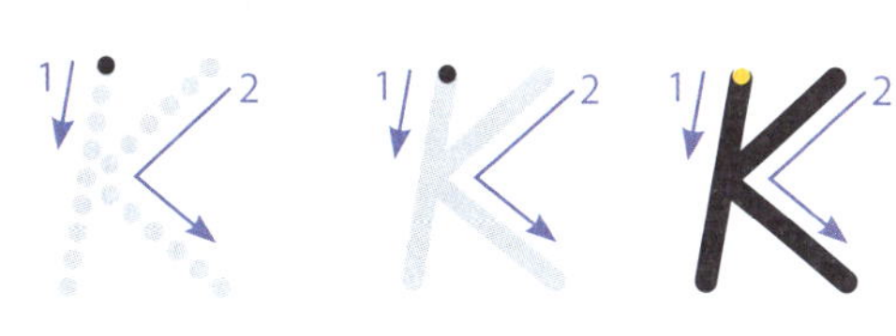

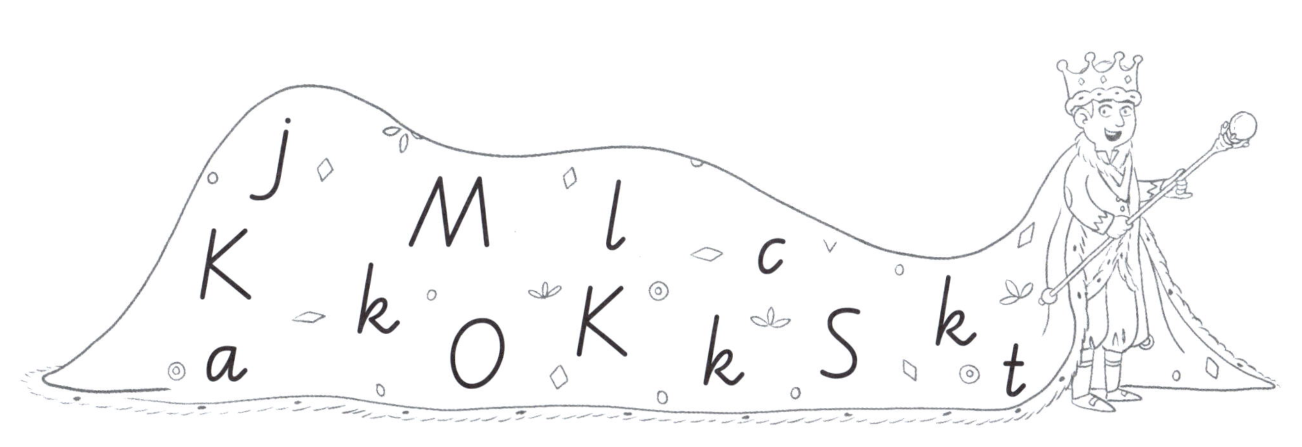

Fast finishers

Circle the lower-case k's on the king's train, and then colour in the king's train.

Track

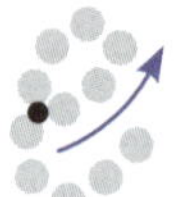     

Trace

Copy

Self-assessment!

Ask students to circle their best lower-case e and upper-case E.
Ask them to explain the reason for their choices to you or a classmate.

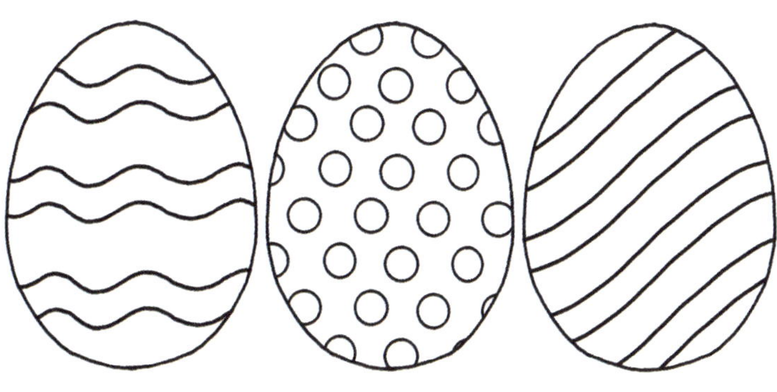

Fast finishers

Trace the word "egg", and then colour in the decorated eggs.

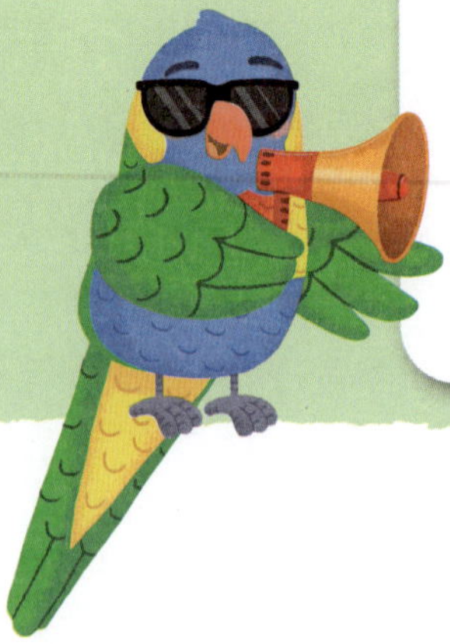

Track

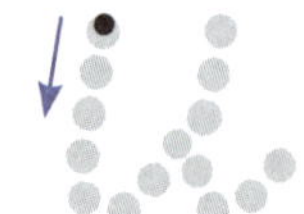

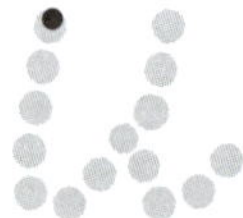

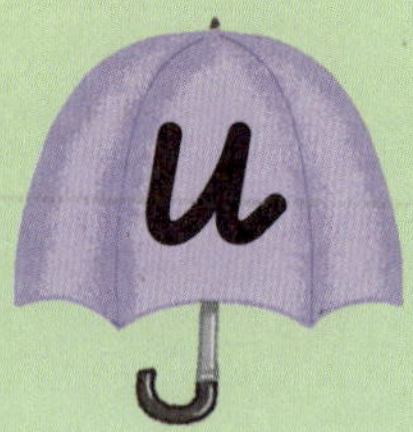

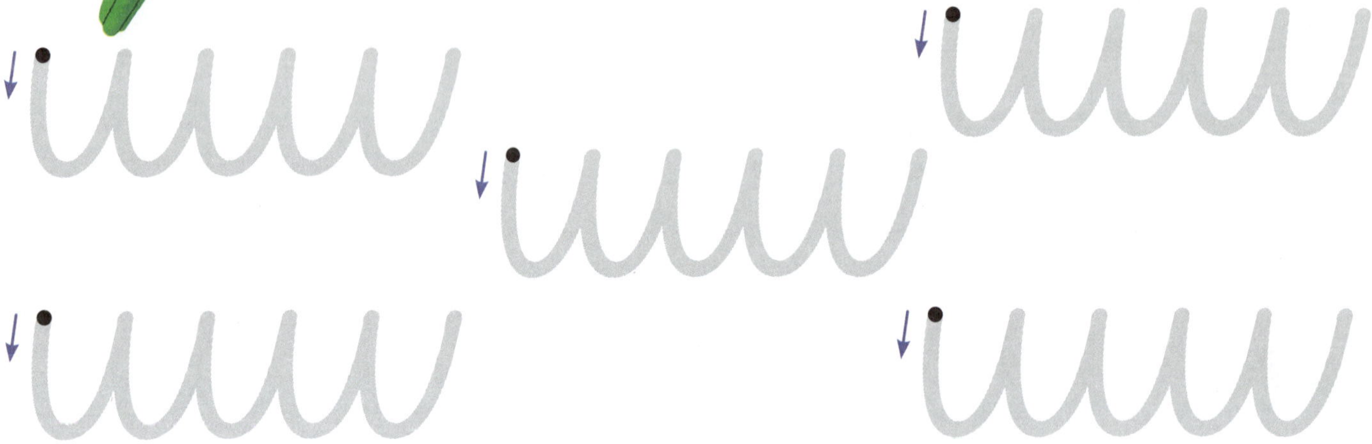

Trace

Copy

u

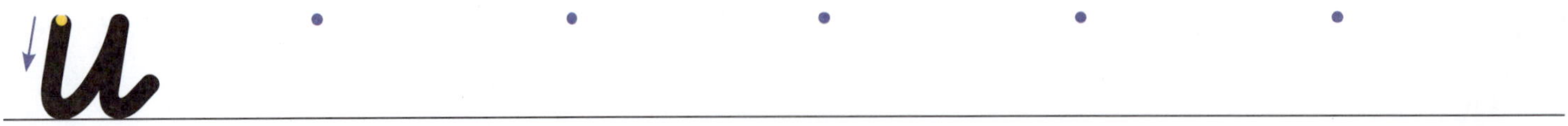

Self-assessment!

Ask students to circle their best lower-case u and upper-case U.
Ask them to explain the reason for their choices to you or a classmate.

u u u

up

Fast finishers

Trace the word "up", and then colour in the arrow. Draw something that goes up. For example, a balloon, a lift or a crane.

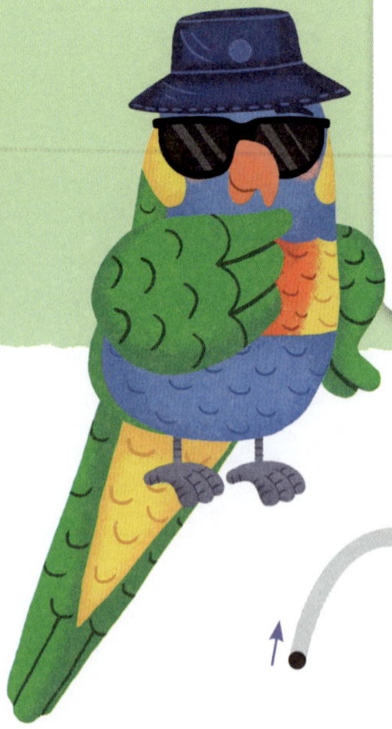

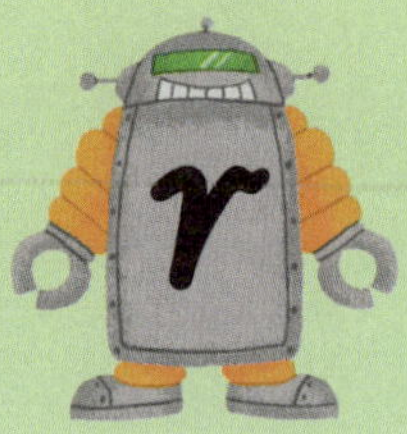

Track

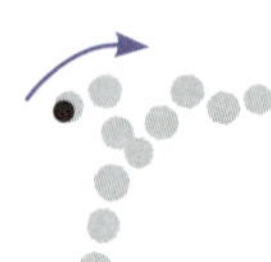  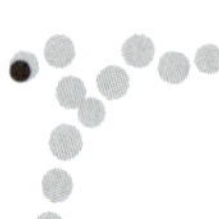  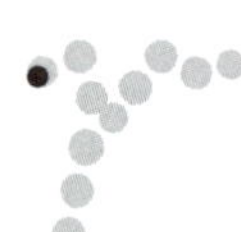 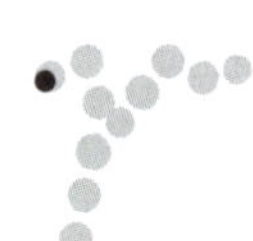

Trace

Copy

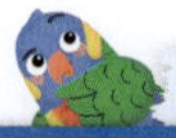

Self-assessment!

Ask students to circle their best lower-case r and upper-case R.
Ask them to explain the reason for their choices to you or a classmate.

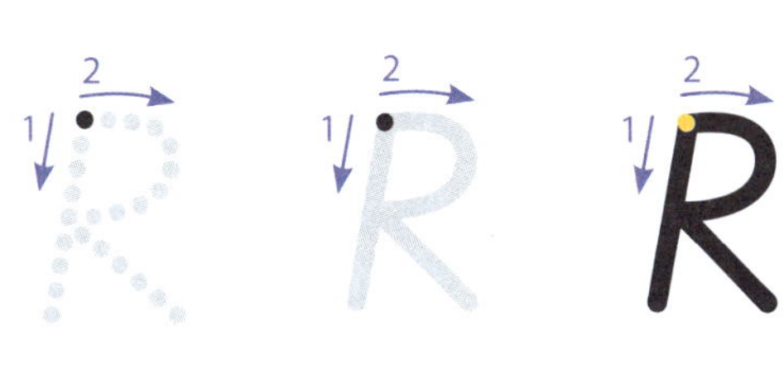

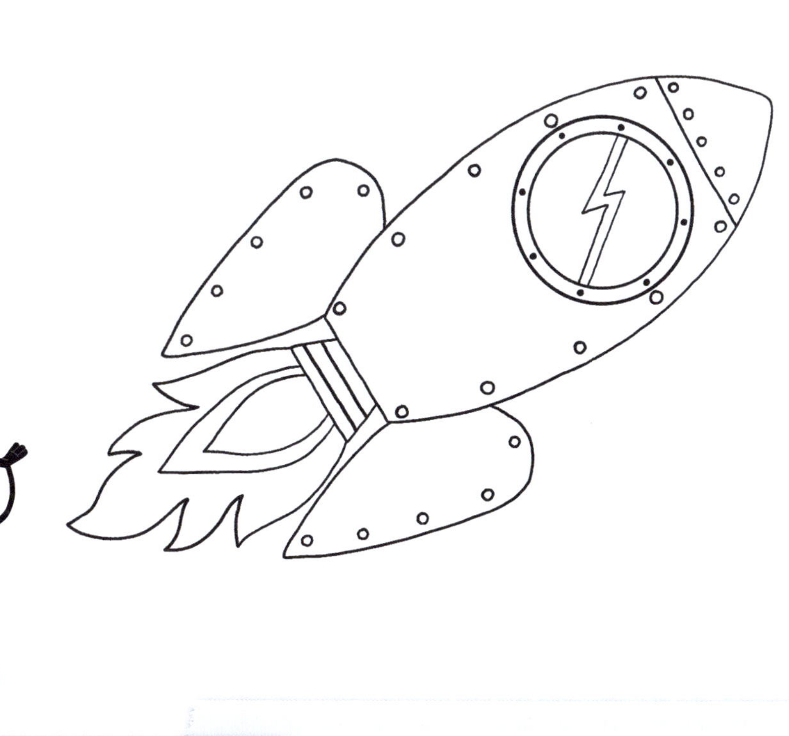

Fast finishers

Colour in the rocket or draw something that begins with the /r/ phoneme (sound).

Track

Trace

Copy

Self-assessment!

Ask students to circle their best lower-case h and upper-case H.
Ask them to explain the reason for their choices to you or a classmate.

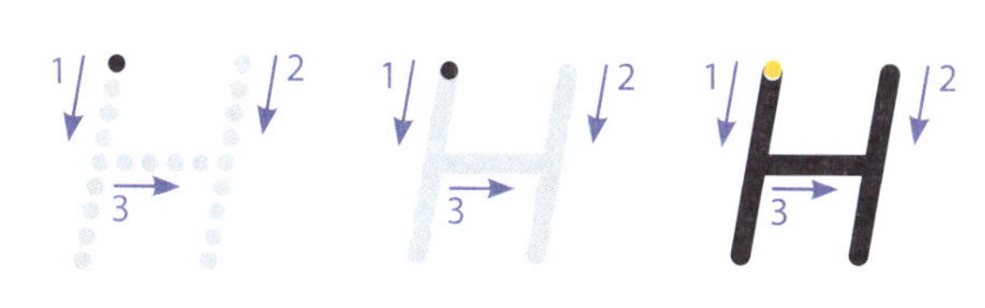

hut

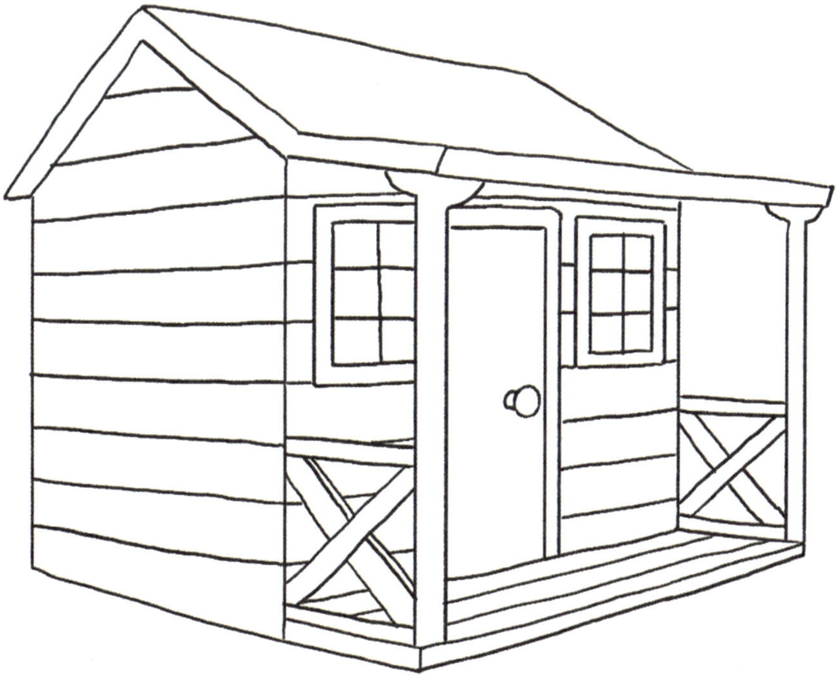

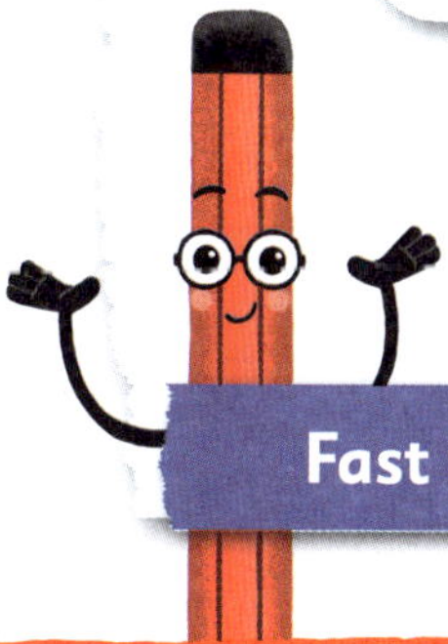

Fast finishers

Trace the word "hut", and then colour in the picture.

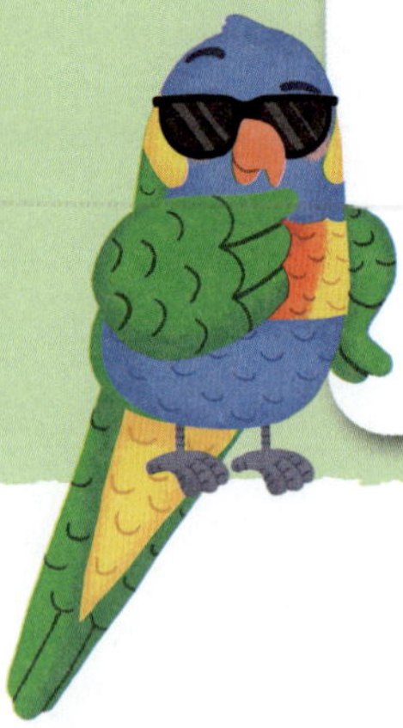

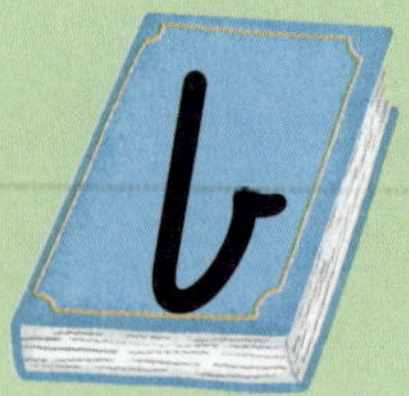

Track

Trace

Copy

Self-assessment!

Ask students to circle their best lower-case b and upper-case B.
Ask them to explain the reason for their choices to you or a classmate.

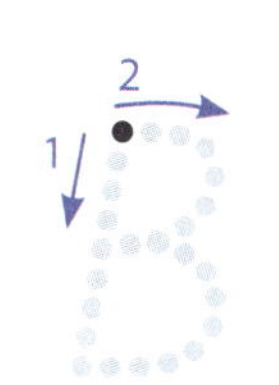

Fast finishers

Put a circle around all the lower-case b's and upper-case B's. Then colour in the flowers.

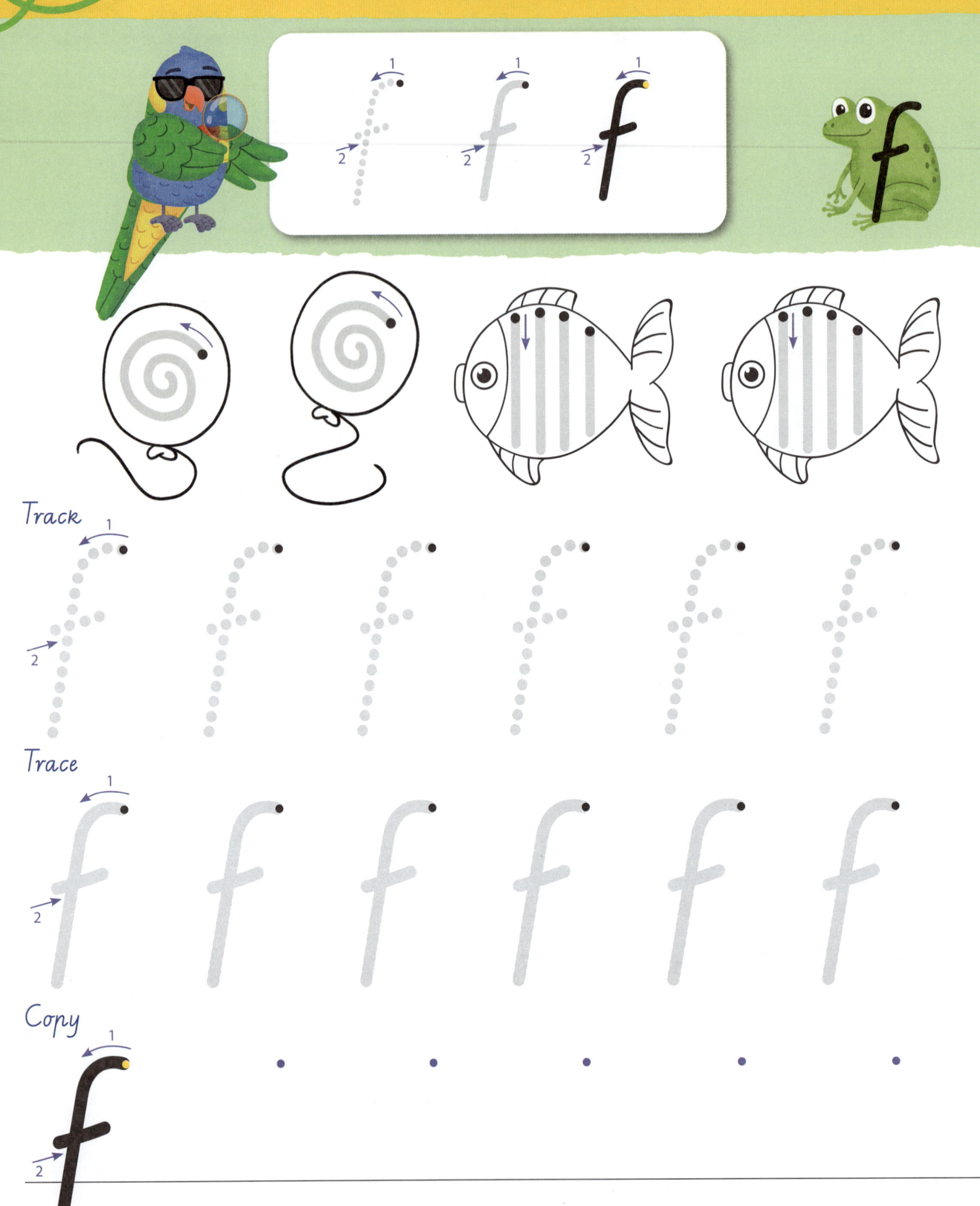

Self-assessment!

Ask students to circle their best lower-case f and upper-case F.
Ask them to explain the reason for their choices to you or a classmate.

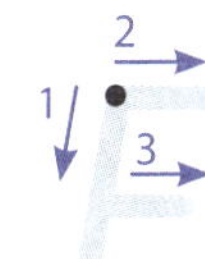

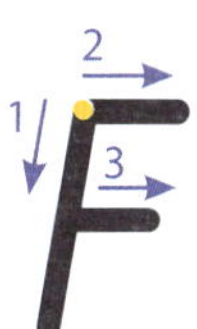

Fast finishers Trace the word "off", and then draw something that can switch on and off.

Track

l l l l l l

Trace

l l l l l l

Copy

l

Self-assessment!

Ask students to circle their best lower-case l and upper-case L.
Ask them to explain the reason for their choices to you or a classmate.

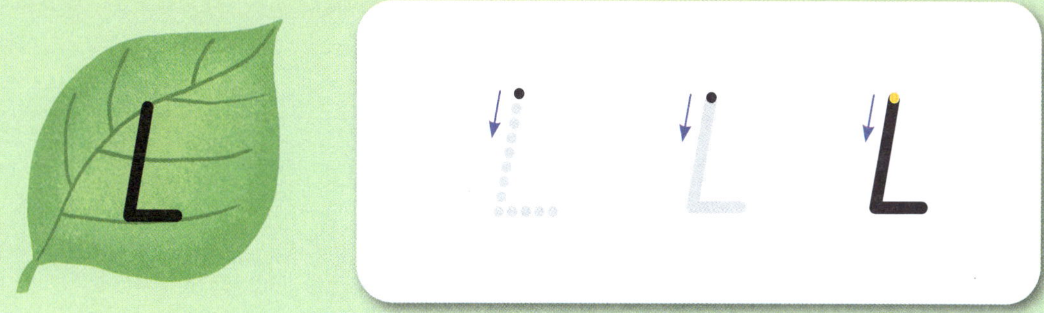

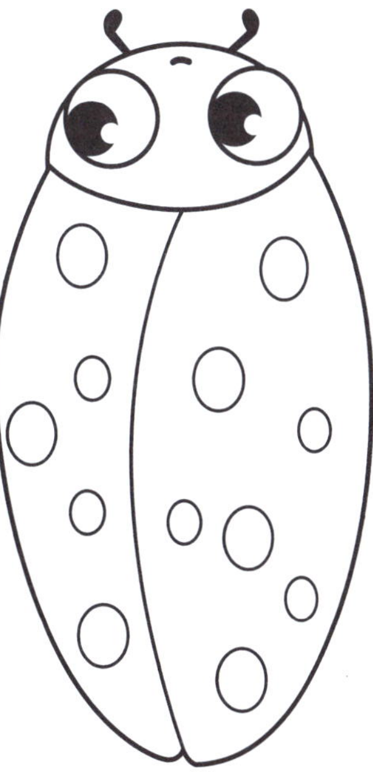

Fast finishers Trace the word "legs". Then add six legs to the ladybird and colour it in.

Track

Trace

Copy

Self-assessment!

Ask students to circle their best lower-case j and upper-case J.
Ask them to explain the reason for their choices to you or a classmate.

Fast finishers

Colour in the jugglers that have a lower-case j on them in one colour. Then colour in the remaining jugglers in different colours.

Track

Trace

Copy

Self-assessment!

Ask students to circle their best lower-case v and upper-case V.
Ask them to explain the reason for their choices to you or a classmate.

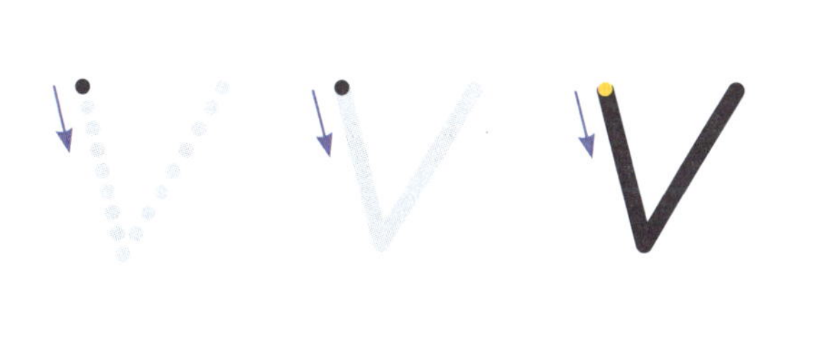

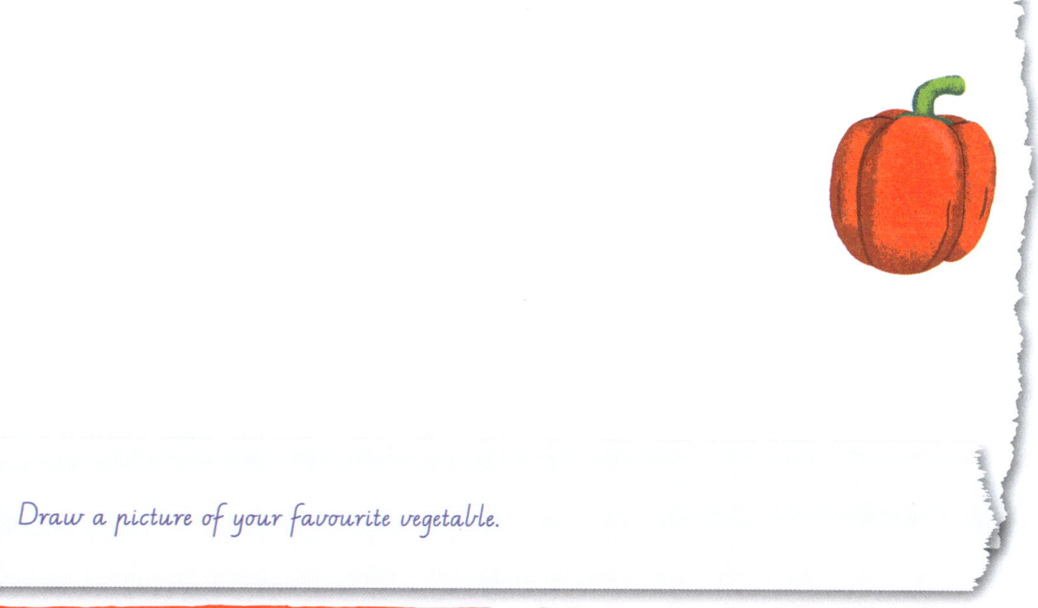

Fast finishers

Draw a picture of your favourite vegetable.

w w w

Track

Trace

Copy

Self-assessment!

Ask students to circle their best lower-case w and upper-case W.
Ask them to explain the reason for their choices to you or a classmate.

Fast finishers

Colour in the watermelons that have a lower-case w inside them in red and green. Then colour in the remaining watermelons in different colours.

Track

Trace

Copy

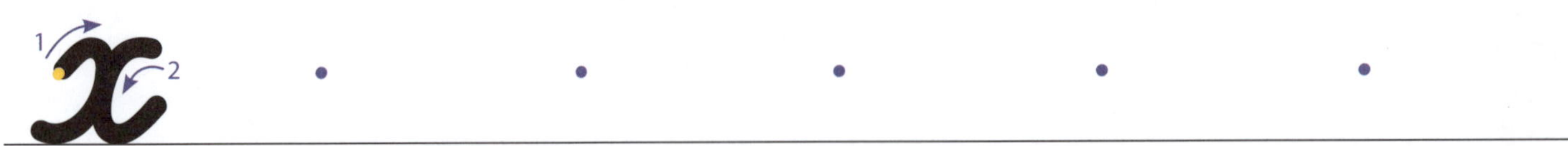

Self-assessment!

Ask students to circle their best lower-case x and upper-case X.
Ask them to explain the reason for their choices to you or a classmate.

above
on
below

above
on
below

above
on
below

above
on
below

Fast finishers

Trace the word "six", and then draw six things. For example, six faces, six bugs or six cups.

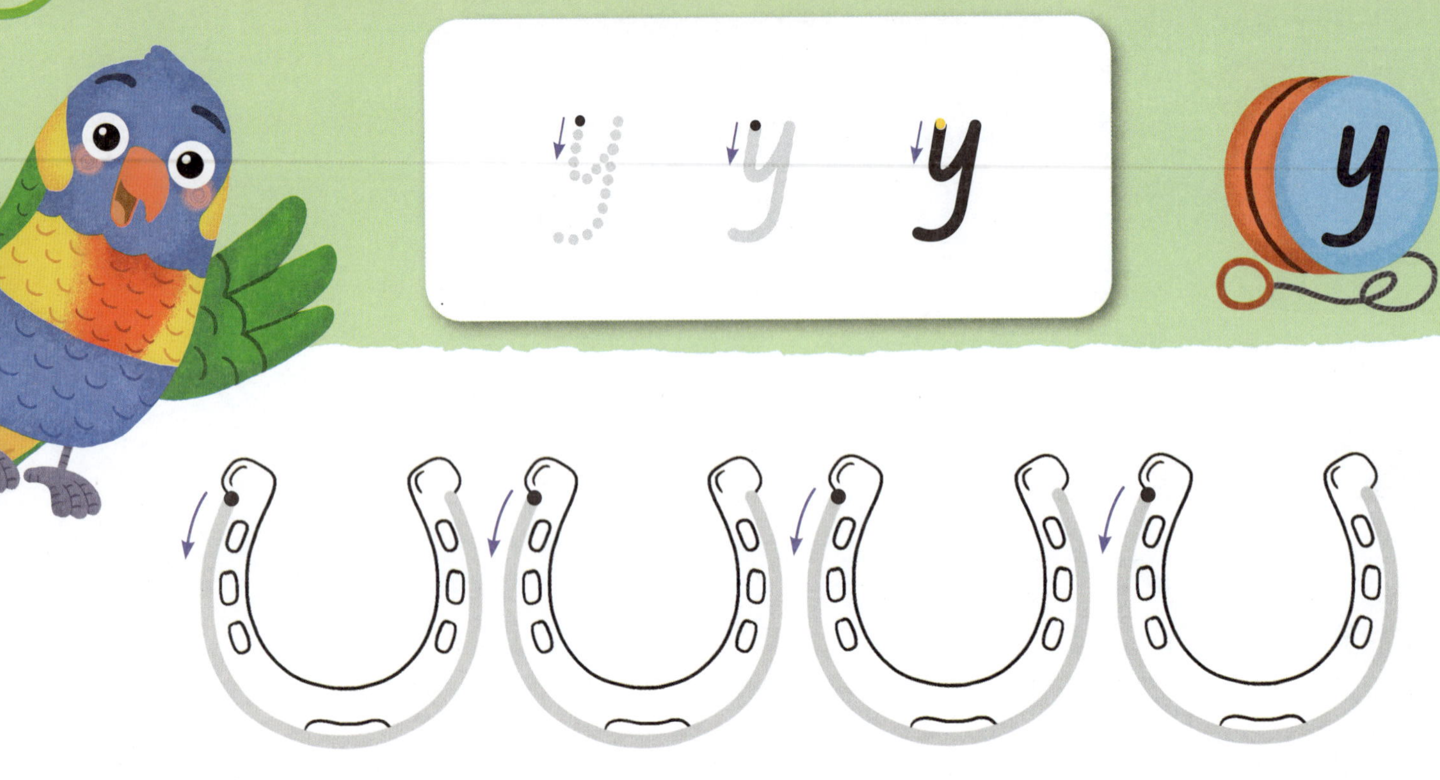

Track

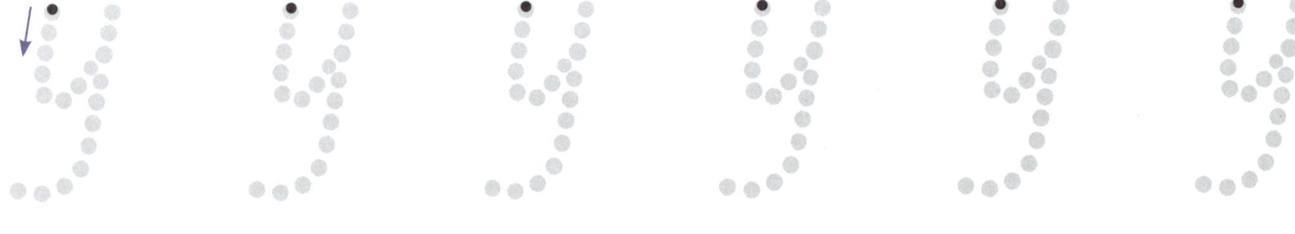

Trace

Copy

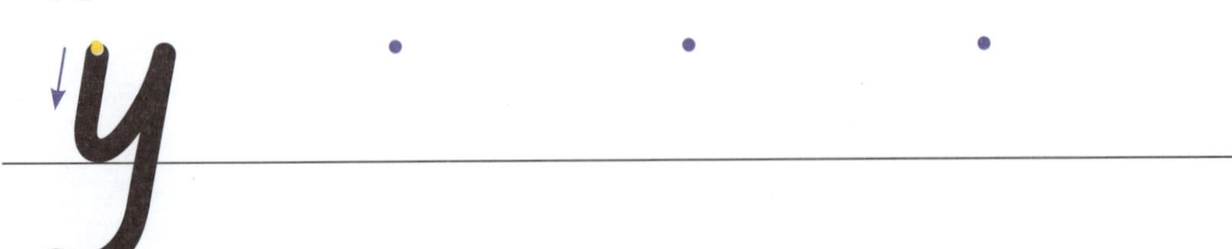

Self-assessment!

Ask students to circle their best lower-case y and upper-case Y.
Ask them to explain the reason for their choices to you or a classmate.

Fast finishers

Circle all the lower-case y's and upper-case Y's. What could you add to this picture? For example, a bird, the Sun or a fish. What could you colour in yellow?

Track

Trace

Copy

Self-assessment!

Ask students to circle their best lower-case ʒ and upper-case Z.
Ask them to explain the reason for their choices to you or a classmate.

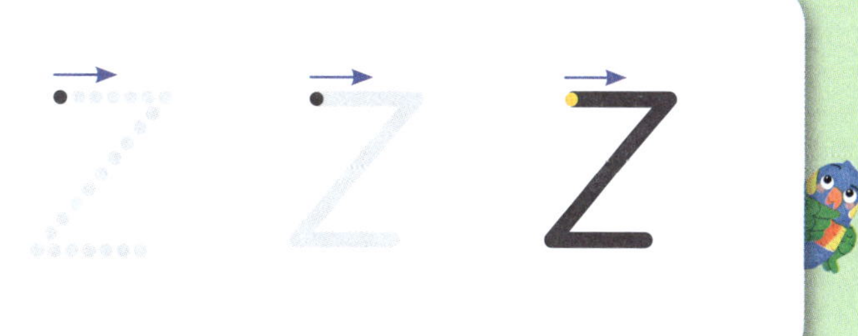

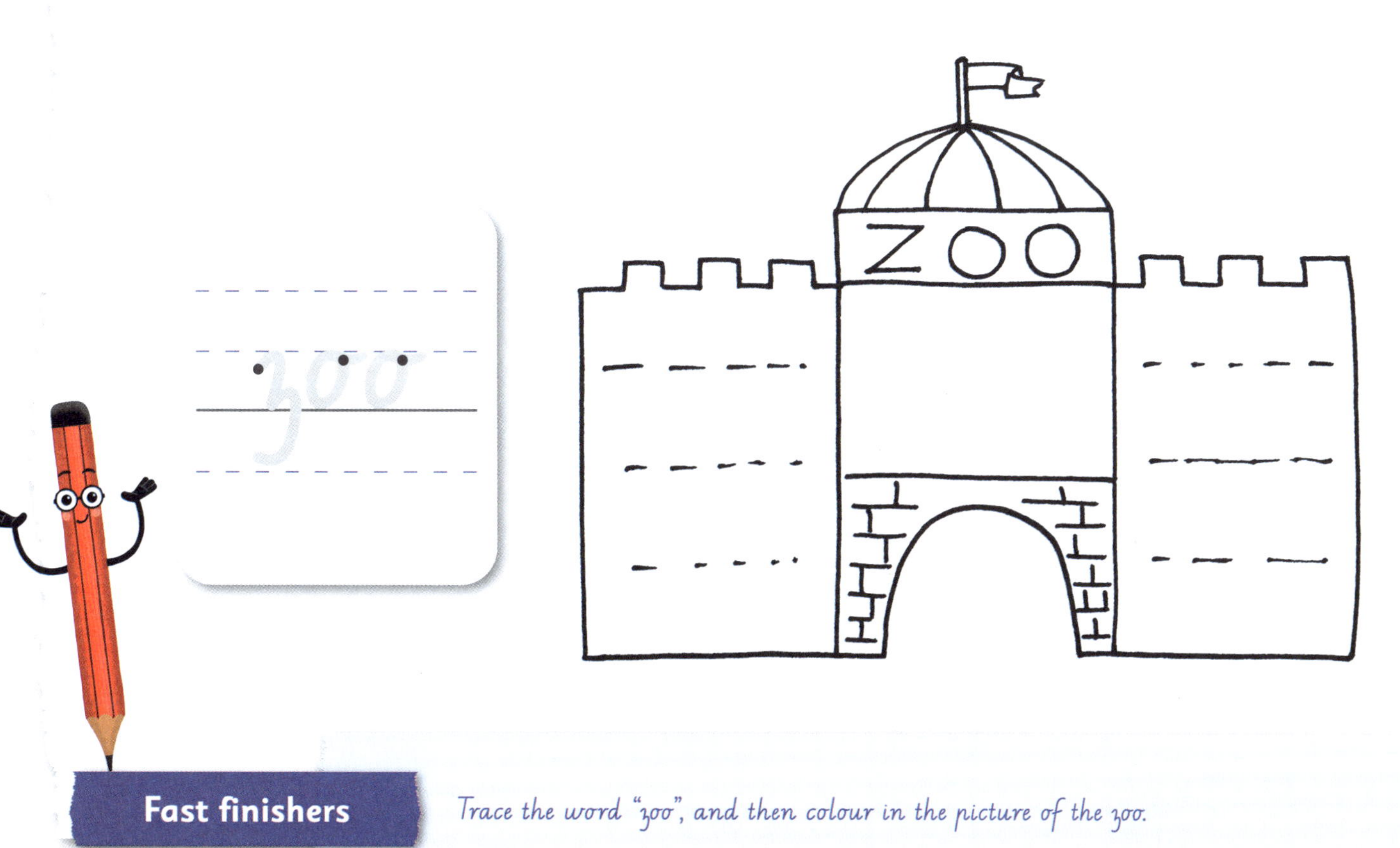

Fast finishers *Trace the word "zoo", and then colour in the picture of the zoo.*

Track

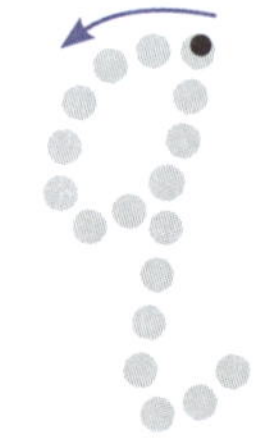     

Trace

Copy

Self-assessment!

Ask students to circle their best lower-case q and upper-case Q.
Ask them to explain the reason for their choices to you or a classmate.

Fast finishers Trace the word "quack", and then draw a duck.

Number practice

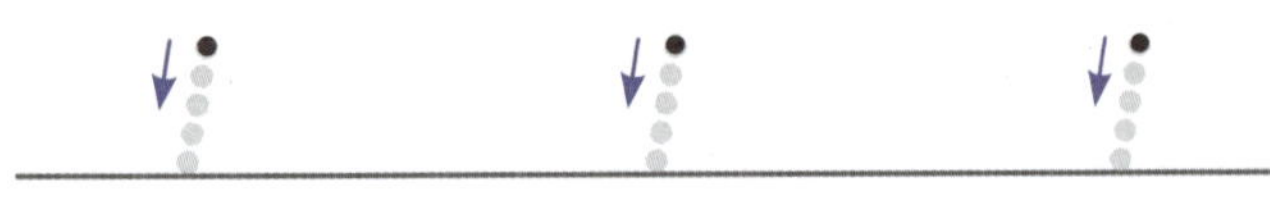

1

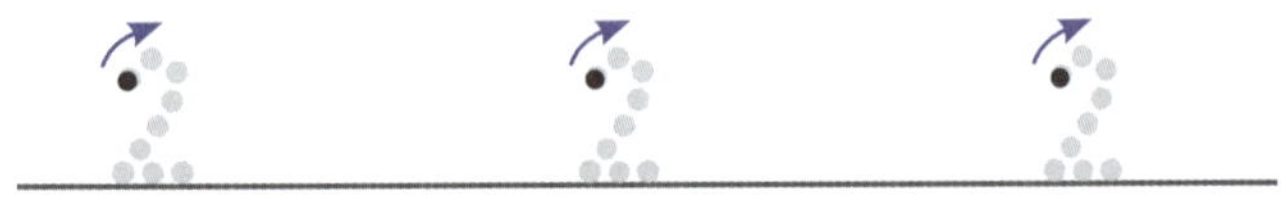

2

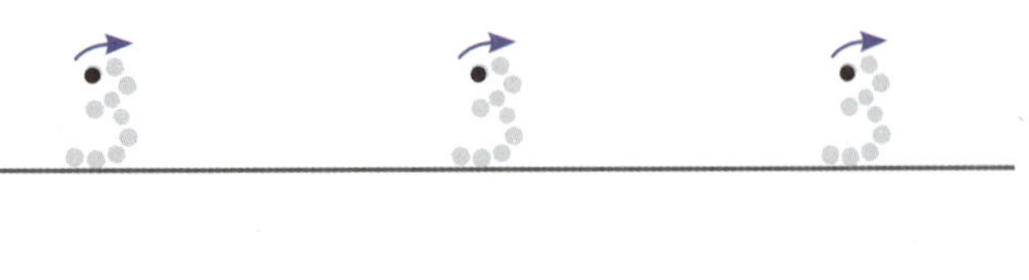

3

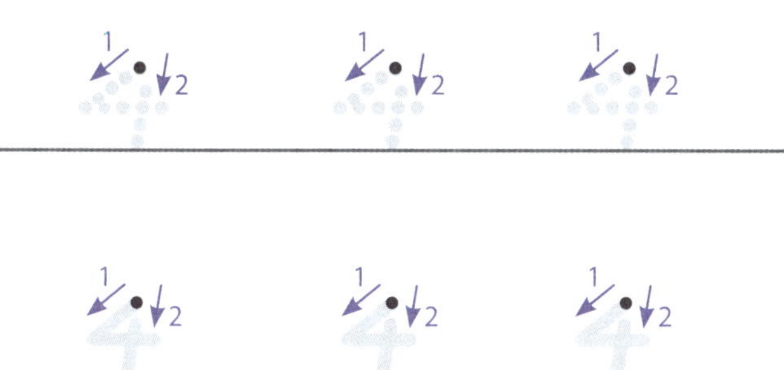

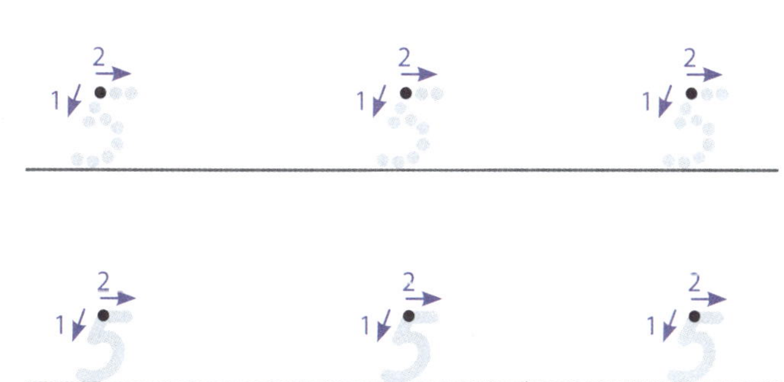

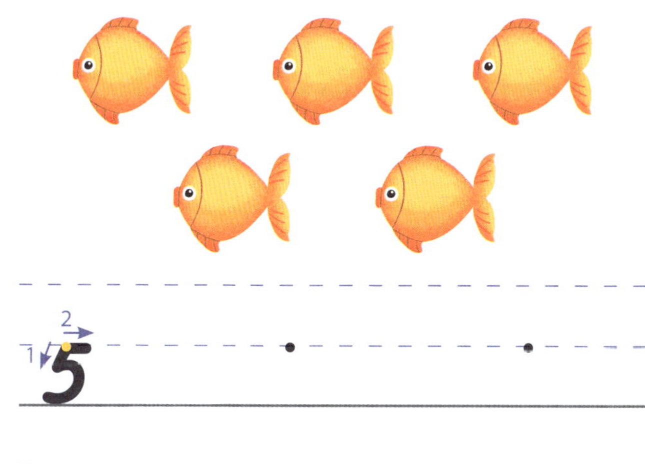

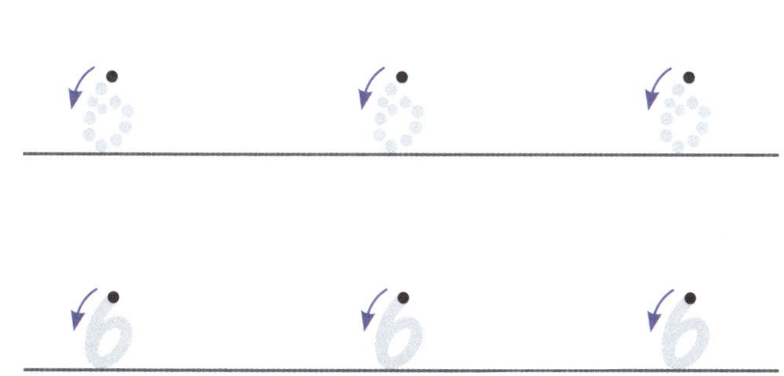

10

Fast finishers

Choose your favourite number, and then draw a picture with that number of animals.

Alphabet

a b c d e f g h i

j k l m n o p q r

s t u v w x y z

A B C D E F G H I

J K L M N O P Q R

S T U V W X Y Z